READING ABOUT

Going to School

By Jim Pipe

Aladdin/Watts
London • Sydney

At school

2

It is the first day of school.
"I've got butterflies in my tummy," says Alex.

"Don't worry!" says Mum.
"I'll help you get ready."

Getting ready

3

"Am I late?" asks Alex.

Packing
the bag

"Don't worry," says Mum.

"We'll get to school on time."

4

"Did you pack my pencils and crayons?" asks Alex.

"Don't worry! I packed them in your bag," says Mum. "Let's go!"

Pencil case

Crayons

Pencils

Rubber

Ruler

On the way, Alex sees lots of other children. They wave to each other.

"Will I know anyone?" asks Alex.

"Don't worry!" says Mum.
"Look, there's your friend Sally."

Sally is at the gate with her mum.

School gate

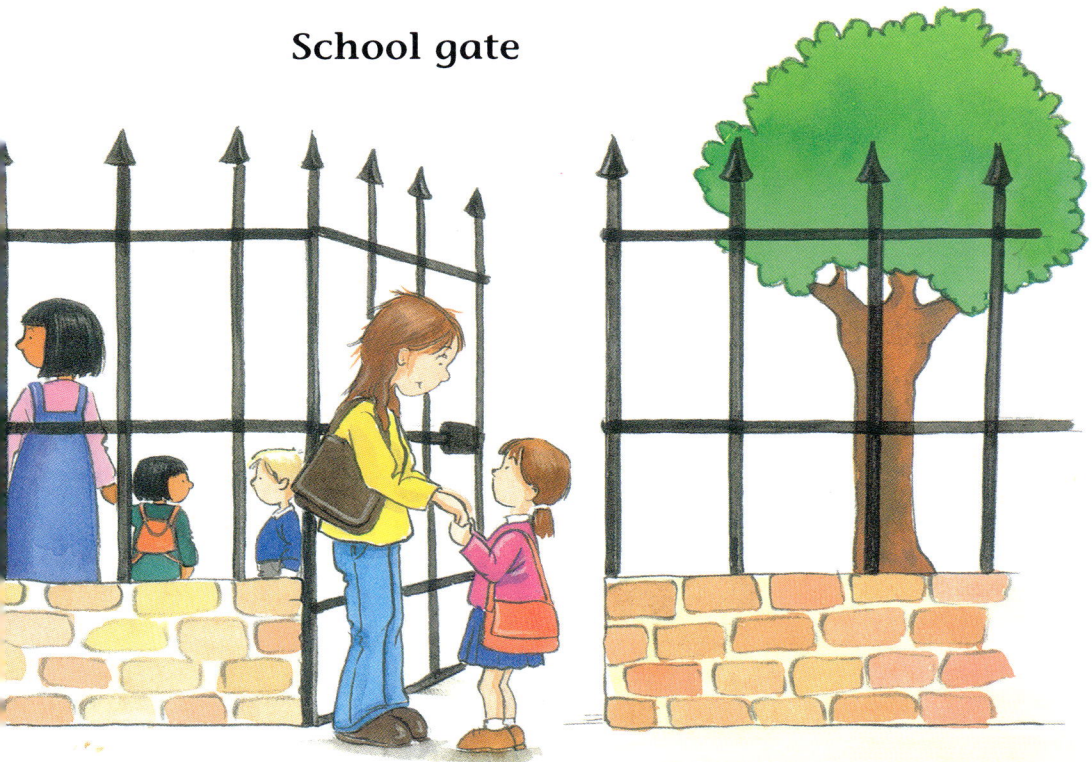

Sally and Alex walk to the classroom with their mums.

"Look at all the things to do," says Alex's mum.

"Yes," says Alex. "This will be fun!"

"See you later," says Mum.

Classroom

The teacher is called Mr Adams.

"Good morning," he says.

"Sit down," says Mr Adams.

"Let's do some writing."

Sitting down

"I forgot my letters," says Sally.

"Don't worry!" whispers Alex.

"We can learn together."

"A is in apple," says Mr Adams,
"and B is in…"
"Banana!" shouts Alex.

"Very good," laughs Mr Adams.

Putting up a hand

Soon it is lunch time.

Alex and Sally see a boy
eating on his own.

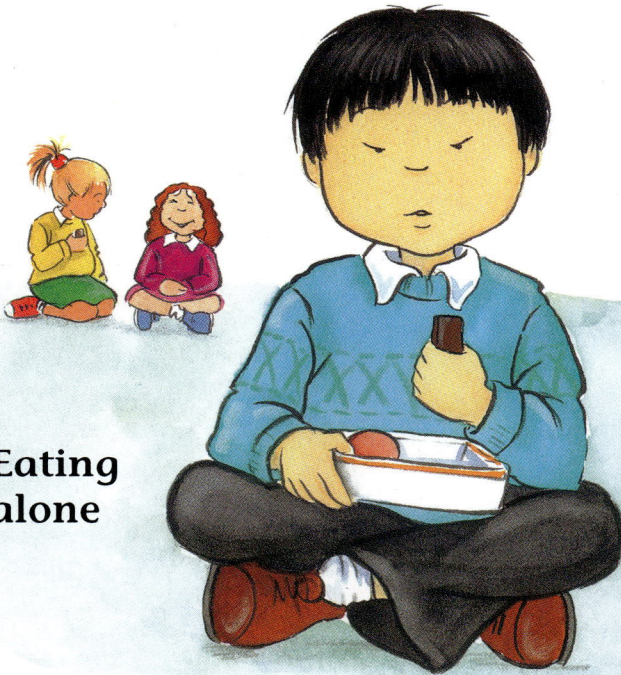

Eating
alone

"Hi," says Alex.

"What's your name?"

"I'm Jin Soo," says the boy.

"Would you like some food from my lunch box?"

Lunch box

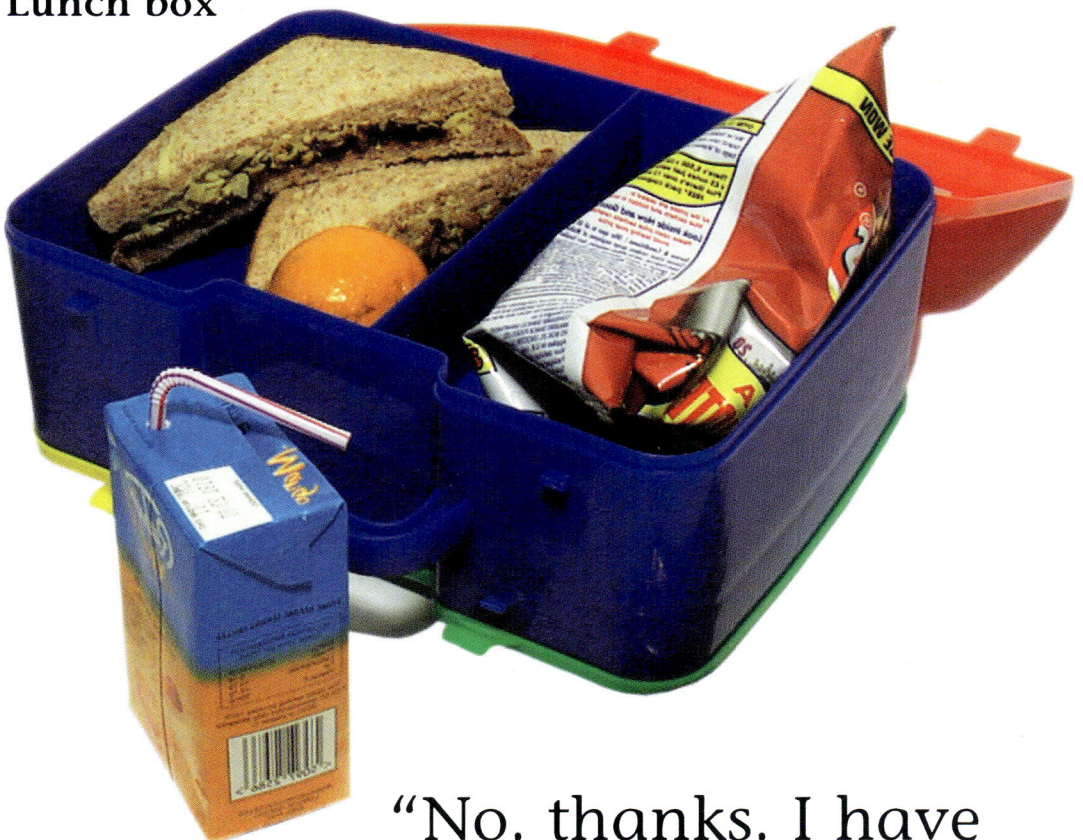

"No, thanks, I have my own," says Alex.

"I don't know anyone," says Jin Soo.

"Don't worry!" says Sally.

"Come and play with us."

In the playground

So Jin Soo plays with Sally and Alex in the playground.

"This is great fun," says Jin Soo.

After lunch, it is time to paint.
"My brush is too stiff," says Alex.

"Don't worry," says Jin Soo.
"You can use pens
or crayons."

Crayons

So Alex draws a picture
with his pens.

Brush

"Very good, Alex," says Mr Adams.
Jin Soo smiles at Alex.

Paints

After painting, it is story time. "I love stories," says Sally.

At the end, everyone gets ready to go home.

Story time

Dad meets Alex at the gate. "Did you have a good time at school?"

"Yes. I made a new friend, Jin Soo!" Alex waves goodbye to his friends.

Waving goodbye

At home, Mum is waiting.

"Look at my picture," says Alex.
"It's a present for you."

Picture

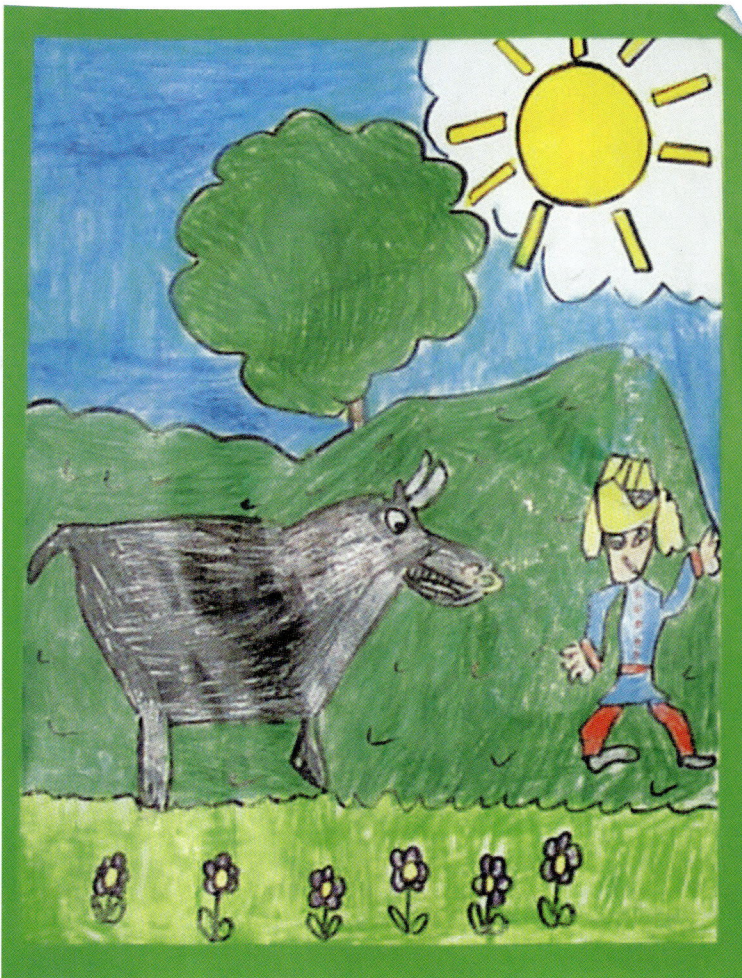

"Thanks," says Mum. "Where are your butterflies now?" Alex smiles and says, "All gone!"

Here are some words and phrases from the book.

Pack your bag

Put up a hand

In the classroom

Eat lunch

Wave goodbye

Paint a picture

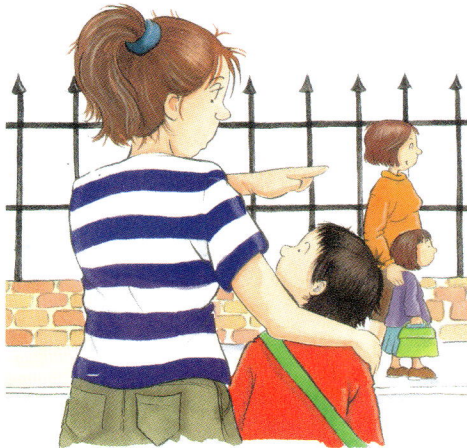

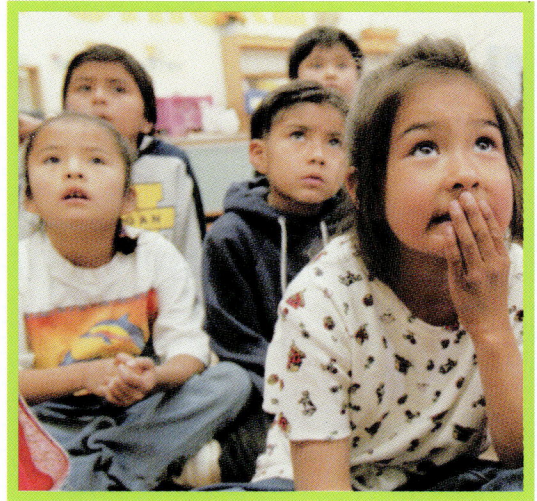

Arrive at school

Hear a story

Can you use these words to write your own story?

Did you see these in the book?

Slide

Pencil sharpener

Crisps

Globe

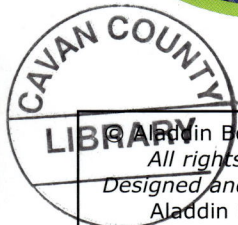

© Aladdin Books Ltd 2001
All rights reserved
Designed and produced by
Aladdin Books Ltd
28 Percy Street
London W1T 2BZ
Literacy Consultant
Phil Whitehead
Printed in U.A.E.

*First published in
Great Britain in 2001 by*
Franklin Watts
96 Leonard Street
London EC2A 4XD
*A catalogue record for this
book is available from the
British Library.*
ISBN 0 7496 4840 6

Illustrator
Mary Lonsdale - SGA
Painting page 20: J. Eskdale
Picture Credits
All photos by Select Pictures
except 8-9, 24br -
Catherine Karnow/CORBIS;
10 - Corbis; 18, 23, 24br -
Kevin Fleming/CORBIS.